International
Cooking Collection

Seasonal Soups
& Appetizers

International
Cooking Collection

Seasonal Soups
& Appetizers
Mary Cadogan

CONTENTS

Spring   6

Summer   24

Fall   42

Winter   60

Stocks & Accompaniments   78

Index   80

Published exclusively for Cupress (Canada) Ltd
20 Torbay Road, Markham, Ontario L3R 1G6 Canada
by Woodhead-Faulkner (Publishers) Ltd, Simon & Schuster International Group

This edition first published 1988
© Woodhead-Faulkner (Publishers) Ltd 1988
All rights reserved
ISBN 0-920691-49-8
Printed and bound in Italy

INTRODUCTION

This book isn't simply a collection of first-course recipes. I love appetizers so much, with their tantalizing promise of what is to come, that I often serve two, or even three, and forget a main course completely. I may start with a soup or a creamy dip, go on to a vegetable or salad, then follow with a more substantial appetizer. I find appetizers offer so much scope for pretty presentation.

Alternatively you could make several appetizers to serve together, buffet-style. For dishes to serve with drinks, try Herbed Yogurt Cheese with Radishes and Garlic Toast, Fried Potato Skins or Pakoras with Fresh Mint Chutney.

I have grouped the recipes into seasons to help you enjoy fresh produce when it is at its best, most flavorsome and often cheapest. Having so much produce from around the world to choose from has blurred the seasons a bit, giving us such things as strawberries at Christmastime. But as each season arrives, it still brings special pleasures. There's nothing quite like the taste of the first home-grown tomatoes and bunches of radishes to herald summer.

As the days draw in, the fall tones of golds and reds are reflected in pumpkins and squashes of all shapes and sizes, sweet red-skinned onions and an array of nuts in their shells. Try Pumpkin Soup to keep out the first chill.

Root vegetables still belong firmly to winter—parsnips, celeriac and rutabaga conjure up images of heart-warming soups and creamy purees. My favorite soups are Spiced Parsnip and Carrot and Celeriac.

Spring brings with it a feeling of renewal, and the root crops make way for the more delicate flavors of young spinach leaves, tiny new carrots, tender lettuces and the first fresh herbs. Carrot and Herb Salad is simply sweet new carrots flavored with fresh herbs.

Try out these recipes, whatever the season. Try them on family, friends or just for yourself. But please, above all, eat and enjoy them.

NOTES

All spoon measurements are level.

Ovens should be preheated to the temperature specified.

Freshly ground black pepper is intended where pepper is listed.

Fresh herbs are used unless otherwise stated. If unobtainable dried herbs can be substituted in cooked dishes but halve the quantities.

Use U.S. grade large eggs unless otherwise stated.

Basic stocks and accompaniments are marked with an asterisk and given in the reference section (pages 78–9).

SPRING VEGETABLES WITH WARM MINT DRESSING

The vegetables I have suggested here can be varied according to the season, but they must always be perfectly fresh as their individual flavors are so important in this simple dish.

¼ lb broccoli
¼ lb green beans
⅓ lb baby carrots
½ cup snow peas
1–2 small cooked beets, sliced thinly
few radicchio leaves
½ lb tiny thin-skinned potatoes, boiled in their skins

FOR THE DRESSING:
¼ cup sweet butter
4 scallions, chopped
1 tablespoon chopped mint
⅔ cup Vegetable Stock*
6 tablespoons dry white wine
⅔ cup whipping cream
salt and pepper to taste

Serves 4
Preparation time:
30 minutes
Cooking time:
6 minutes
Freezing:
Not recommended

1. Break the broccoli into small florets. Peel and thinly slice the stalks. Cook the broccoli, beans and carrots together in boiling salted water for 5 minutes. Add the snow peas and cook for 1 minute. Drain and cool quickly under cold running water.
2. Arrange all the vegetables in small groups on 4 individual plates.
3. Melt 1 tablespoon of the butter in a saucepan, add the scallions and mint and cook for about 1 minute.
4. Add the stock, wine and cream and bring to the boil, stirring constantly. Simmer until reduced by a third, then stir in the remaining butter, a teaspoon at a time, until the sauce is thickened and glossy. Season with pepper, and salt if necessary. Keep warm.
5. Just before serving, pour the warm sauce over the vegetables.

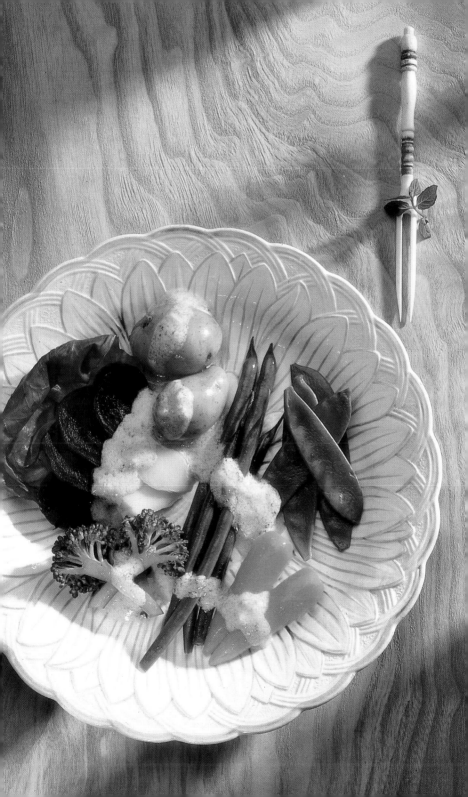

ZUCCHINI AND HAM STIR-FRY

2 tablespoons butter
1 teaspoon salad oil
1 clove garlic, chopped
  finely
1 lb zucchini, cut into thin
  sticks

¹/₄ lb ham, cut into strips
3 tablespoons whipping
  cream
salt and pepper to taste

Serves 4
Preparation time:
10 minutes
Cooking time:
5 minutes
Freezing:
Not recommended

1. Melt the butter and oil in a frying pan, add the garlic and fry for a few seconds. Add the zucchini and cook, stirring, for about 2 minutes, until just softened. Stir in the ham and heat through.
2. Lower the heat and stir in the cream, and salt and pepper. Serve piping hot, with soft warm bread for mopping up the juices.

ZUCCHINI SOUFFLÉS

These light airy soufflés make a surprisingly filling appetizer.

¹/₄ cup butter
2 cups grated zucchini
¹/₄ cup all-purpose flour
²/₃ cup milk
1 teaspoon chopped
  tarragon

¹/₂ cup grated Gruyère
  cheese
3 eggs, separated
salt and pepper to taste
tarragon sprigs to garnish

Serves 4
Preparation time:
30 minutes
Cooking time:
25 minutes
Freezing:
Not recommended

1. Melt half of the butter in a small pan, add the zucchini and fry gently until softened. Remove from the heat.
2. Melt the remaining butter in a saucepan, add the flour and cook for 1 minute. Gradually stir in the milk, until thickened and smooth.
3. Remove from the heat and stir in the zucchini, tarragon, cheese, egg yolks, and salt and pepper. Beat the egg whites until stiff, then fold carefully into the zucchini mixture.
4. Divide between 4 greased 1¹/₄ cup ovenproof dishes and bake in a 375°F oven for 25 minutes, until well risen and browned. Serve immediately, garnished with tarragon sprigs.

CARROT AND HERB SALAD

The beauty of this recipe is its simplicity, but to succeed it must be made with only the youngest and sweetest carrots and the freshest herbs.

3 cups grated carrot
1 teaspoon lemon juice
1 tablespoon chopped
  mixed herbs, e.g. chervil,
  tarragon, mint, parsley

2 tablespoons snipped
  chives
1 teaspoon Dijon mustard
3 tablespoons olive oil
salt and pepper to taste

Serves 4
Preparation time:
15 minutes
Freezing:
Not recommended

1. Pile the carrot onto 4 individual plates. Place the lemon juice, herbs, mustard, and salt and pepper in a bowl and mix well. Stir in the olive oil.
2. Just before serving, spoon the dressing over the carrots.

SMOKED MACKEREL AND ORANGE SALAD

The tiny alfalfa sprouts go particularly well with smoked mackerel and orange, but if you cannot obtain them use beansprouts instead.

2 oranges
2 heads Belgium endive,
  shredded
2 cups alfalfa sprouts
1 Boston lettuce
1/2 lb smoked mackerel,
  skinned and flaked

2 teaspoons creamed
  horseradish
3 tablespoons plain yogurt
salt and pepper to taste
orange slices to garnish

Serves 4
Preparation time:
15 minutes
Freezing:
Not recommended

1. Peel the oranges, discarding all pith. Cut into segments over a small bowl to catch the juice; set the juice aside. Cut each orange segment in half and place in a bowl with the Belgium endive and alfalfa sprouts. Mix well.
2. Arrange the lettuce on 4 individual plates and spoon the Belgium endive mixture in the center. Top with the smoked mackerel.
3. Place 1 tablespoon of the reserved orange juice in a bowl, add the horseradish, yogurt, and salt and pepper and beat together with a fork.
4. Drizzle a little dressing over each salad and garnish with orange slices to serve.

WILTED SPINACH AND EGG SALAD

2 eggs
¾ lb young spinach leaves,
    shredded
8 radishes, sliced
1 avocado, peeled and
    chopped
4 tablespoons salad oil

2 shallots, chopped
4 strips bacon, chopped
1 teaspoon Dijon mustard
1 tablespoon white wine
    vinegar
pepper to taste

1. Boil the eggs for 5 minutes, then shell and cool quickly.
Cut each one in half.
2. Divide the spinach between 4 individual plates and top
with the radishes, avocado and egg.
3. Heat 1 tablespoon of the oil in a small saucepan, add the
shallots and bacon and fry for about 5 minutes, until the
bacon is crisp. Lower the heat and stir in the mustard,
vinegar, pepper and remaining oil. Pour evenly over each
salad. Serve immediately.

Serves 4
Preparation time:
30 minutes
Freezing:
Not recommended

SMOKED SALMON AND ASPARAGUS TERRINE

¹/₂ lb smoked salmon	1 tablespoon snipped
¹/₂ lb asparagus, cooked	chives
lightly	2 tablespoons butter,
1 cup curd cheese or	melted
farmer's cheese	1 tablespoon lemon juice
1 teaspoon chopped	salt and pepper to taste
tarragon	lettuce leaves to garnish

Serves 4–6
Preparation time:
35 minutes, plus
chilling
Freezing:
Recommended

1. Line a 7¹/₂ × 3¹/₂ × 2¹/₂ inch loaf pan with smoked salmon, trimming the edges to neaten, but leaving enough to fold over the finished terrine. Set aside 3 asparagus spears.

2. Chop the remaining smoked salmon and asparagus, place in a food processor or blender and work together until fairly smooth. Add the remaining ingredients and work together until smooth.

3. Spread half of the mixture in the prepared pan and place the reserved asparagus on top, trimming the spears to the length of the pan if necessary. Cover with the remaining mixture and smooth the top.

4. Fold over the smoked salmon and cover with foil. Chill for several hours, or overnight if possible, until firm. Turn out and cut into slices, using a sharp knife. Serve garnished with lettuce leaves.

SORREL ROULADE WITH SHRIMP

Sorrel has a slightly astringent taste that goes well with all fish dishes. It is easy to grow, but if you don't have it, spinach is a good substitute. The roulade and accompanying sauce are delicious served hot or cold.

1 lb sorrel	1 teaspoon fresh basil
pinch of grated nutmeg	1 tablespoon lemon juice
¹/₂ cup grated Gruyère	¹/₃ lb shelled medium-size
cheese	shrimp (thawed if
4 eggs, separated	frozen)
1 lb ripe tomatoes, skinned	1 teaspoon chopped dill
pinch of sugar	salt and pepper to taste
2 tablespoons tomato paste	dill sprigs to garnish

1. Grease and line a 13 × 9 inch jelly roll pan.
2. Cook the sorrel in a covered pan with just the water

clinging to the leaves after washing for about 5 minutes, until just wilted. Drain well, pressing out as much water as possible. Chop finely, then mix with the nutmeg, cheese, egg yolks, and salt and pepper.

3. Beat the egg whites until stiff, fold into the sorrel mixture, then transfer to the prepared pan; shake to level the mixture. Cook in a 375°F oven for about 15 minutes, until firm.

4. Meanwhile, place the tomatoes, sugar, tomato paste, basil, lemon juice, and salt and pepper in a pan. Simmer, uncovered, for about 10 minutes, until pulpy. Press through a sieve, then mix half with the shrimp and dill. Keep both sauces warm.

5. Invert the roulade onto a sheet of waxed paper. Carefully remove the lining paper, then spread the shrimp mixture over the roulade. Roll up carefully from a short end, using the paper to help you.

6. Cut into slices and arrange on individual plates. Spoon over a little tomato sauce and garnish with dill.

Serves 4–6
Preparation time:
45 minutes
Cooking time:
About 15 minutes
Freezing:
Not recommended

CREAMY SHRIMP POTS

Oyster mushrooms are very tender and need only the briefest cooking time.

¹/₃ lb shelled medium-size shrimp (thawed if necessary)
¹/₂ teaspoon paprika
2 teaspoons cornstarch
2 tablespoons butter

¹/₂ lb oyster mushrooms, halved if large
²/₃ cup sour cream
1 tablespoon breadcrumbs
1 tablespoon grated Parmesan cheese
salt and pepper to taste

Serves 4
Preparation time:
10 minutes
Cooking time:
About 5 minutes
Freezing:
Not recommended

1. Mix together the shrimp, paprika and cornstarch. Melt the butter in a saucepan, add the shrimp and fry, stirring, until heated through.
2. Add the mushrooms and stir-fry for 1 minute. Add the sour cream, and salt and pepper and heat through gently, stirring constantly.
3. Divide the mixture between 4 ramekin dishes. Mix together the breadcrumbs and cheese and sprinkle over the top. Broil for about 2 minutes, until the top is crisp and golden. Serve hot.

SOLE ROLL-UPS WITH ALMOND SAUCE

The almond sauce is Middle Eastern in origin. Its delicate
flavor is perfect with any baked or broiled fish.

4 sole fillets, skinned
3 tablespoons lemon juice
1/2 cup ground almonds
1 1/4 cups Chicken Stock*
1 clove garlic, crushed
1/2 teaspoon turmeric

1 tablespoon chopped
  parsley
salt and pepper to taste
shredded lemon rind to
  garnish

1. Season the sole fillets with salt, pepper and 1
tablespoon of the lemon juice. Roll up and place in a
greased dish. Cover with foil and cook in a 350°F oven for
15–18 minutes, until tender.
2. Meanwhile, prepare the sauce. Place the remaining
lemon juice in a saucepan with the almonds, stock, garlic
and turmeric. Bring to the boil, then simmer for 10
minutes, until thickened. Season with salt and pepper and
stir in the parsley.
3. Divide the sauce between 4 individual warmed plates.
Drain the fish on paper towels and place in the center.
Garnish with lemon rind to serve.

Serves 4
Preparation time:
25 minutes
Cooking time:
15–18 minutes
Freezing:
Not recommended

POTTED HAM WITH PARSLEY

Ideally, this dish should be made the day before it is to be served to allow the flavors to develop. It will keep well in the refrigerator for up to 5 days.

1 lb piece bacon or ham
²/₃ cup dry white wine
2 cloves
few celery leaves
1 small onion, quartered
6 black peppercorns

1 bay leaf
3 parsley sprigs
1 tablespoon lemon juice
2 teaspoons gelatin
¼ cup chopped parsley

Serves 4–6
Preparation time:
25 minutes, plus
chilling
Cooking time:
1½ hours
Freezing:
Not recommended

1. Cut the bacon or ham into 1 inch cubes. Place in a saucepan with the wine, cloves, celery leaves, onion, peppercorns, bay leaf and parsley sprigs. Cover with water and bring to the boil.
2. Skim the surface with a slotted spoon, then cover and simmer for 1½ hours, until the bacon or ham is very tender. Strain, reserving the stock.
3. Flake the bacon or ham finely with a knife and fork and pack into a serving bowl.
4. Measure 1¼ cups of the stock, place in a small pan with the lemon juice and bring to the boil. Remove from the heat and sprinkle over the gelatin, stirring until dissolved. Add half of the chopped parsley, then pour over the bacon or ham. Cool, then chill until set.
5. Sprinkle with the remaining parsley and serve with Country Rusks* and a few salad leaves.

CHICKEN SATÉ

1 lb boneless chicken
breasts, skinned and cut
into thin strips
1 teaspoon turmeric
1 tablespoon lemon juice
salt and pepper to taste
cucumber and onion slices
to serve
FOR THE SAUCE:
1 cup unsweetened flaked
coconut

1½ cups boiling water
2 cloves garlic
1 onion, chopped
2 red chilies, halved, seeded
and chopped roughly
2 tablespoons salad oil
3 tablespoons lemon juice
1 tablespoon light brown
sugar
1 cup ground toasted
peanuts

1. Place the chicken, turmeric, lemon juice, and salt and pepper in a bowl and mix well. Leave to marinate while preparing the sauce.

2. Place the coconut in a bowl, add the water and leave for 5 minutes; strain.

3. Place the garlic, onion, chilies and 1 tablespoon of the coconut water in a food processor or blender and work together until smooth.

4. Heat the oil in a frying pan, add the chili mixture and fry for 2–3 minutes, stirring constantly. Stir in the lemon juice, sugar, remaining coconut water, and salt to taste. Stir well, add the ground peanuts and simmer for 2–3 minutes, until thickened. Remove from the heat, leave to cool, then place in a serving bowl or 4 individual dishes.

5. Thread the chicken onto 16–20 bamboo skewers and broil for 6–8 minutes, turning once, until just cooked. Serve with the peanut sauce and cucumber and onion slices.

Serves 4
Preparation time:
35 minutes
Cooking time:
6–8 minutes
Freezing:
Not recommended

CHILLED ALMOND AND GRAPE SOUP

This soup from southern Spain has a delicate flavor.

¹/₂ cup blanched almonds
4 cloves garlic
1 tablespoon olive oil
1 tablespoon white wine
*   vinegar*
3 cups day-old white
*   bread, crusts removed*

4 cups water or Chicken
*   Stock**
1 tablespoon chopped
*   parsley*
³/₄ lb white grapes, halved
*   and seeded*
salt and pepper to taste
ice cubes to serve

Serves 4
Preparation time:
30 minutes
Freezing:
Not recommended

1. Place the almonds, garlic, oil and vinegar in a food processor or blender and work together until smooth. Add the bread and water or stock, a little at a time, and work until smooth. Season with salt and pepper.
2. Pour into a large serving bowl and stir in the parsley and grapes. Serve in individual bowls, with ice cubes.

SPRING VEGETABLE SOUP WITH PESTO

Mixed vegetable soups are great for using up any leftover vegetables—this list is flexible. Pesto adds just the right touch of zip.

1 tablespoon olive oil
2 strips bacon, chopped
2 leeks, chopped
2 carrots, chopped
2 celery sticks, chopped
1 green pepper, cored,
*   seeded and chopped*

2 oz cauliflower, broken
*   into florets*
1 potato, chopped
14 oz can chopped
*   tomatoes*
4 cups Vegetable Stock*
2 tablespoons pesto
salt and pepper to taste

Serves 4
Preparation time:
25 minutes
Cooking time:
20 minutes
Freezing:
Recommended

1. Heat the oil in a large saucepan, add the bacon and fry for about 5 minutes, until crisp. Add the fresh vegetables and turn in the oil until evenly coated.
2. Stir in the tomatoes and stock. Bring to the boil, cover and simmer for 20 minutes, until the vegetables are tender.
3. Puree one-third of the soup in a food processor, or blender, return to the pan and reheat gently. Season with salt and pepper and stir in the pesto. Serve piping hot with Cheese Sticks*.

BROCCOLI SOUP WITH YOGURT

This soup must be served as soon as it is made as it rapidly loses its fresh taste and color.

1 lb broccoli	*juice of 1 lime*
2 tablespoons butter	*4 cups Chicken Stock**
1 onion, chopped	*²/₃ cup plain yogurt*
1 potato, chopped	*1 tablespoon salad oil*
1 teaspoon grated fresh	*1 teaspoon sesame seeds*
root ginger	*salt and pepper to taste*

Serves 4
Preparation time:
20 minutes
Cooking time:
20–25 minutes
Freezing:
Not recommended

1. Cut the broccoli into florets. Slice the stalks thinly. Set aside a few small florets for garnish.
2. Melt the butter in a large saucepan, add the onion and fry until softened. Add the broccoli, potato and ginger and stir well.
3. Add the lime juice, stock, and salt and pepper. Bring to the boil, then cover and simmer for 20–25 minutes, until the broccoli is tender.
4. Puree in a food processor or blender, return to the pan and reheat gently. Check the seasoning. Carefully stir in the yogurt and heat through, making sure the soup does not boil.
5. Meanwhile, heat the oil in a small pan, add the reserved broccoli and stir-fry for 2 minutes. Sprinkle with the sesame seeds and stir well.
6. Transfer the soup to 4 individual warmed bowls and top with the broccoli florets. Serve immediately.

MALAYSIAN SHRIMP SOUP

The hot, spicy and sour flavors in this soup will certainly make taste buds tingle. Serve it as part of a spicy meal.

1 lb uncooked large	*2 tablespoons lemon juice*
shrimp	*2 tablespoons finely*
1 tablespoon salad oil	*chopped scallion*
5 cups boiling water	*1 red chili, seeded and*
2 cloves garlic, crushed	*chopped finely*
2 stalks lemon grass	*1 tablespoon chopped*
(optional)	*cilantro leaves*
2 tablespoons chili sauce	*salt to taste*
1 tablespoon lime juice	

1. Shell the shrimp and reserve the heads. Cut the shrimp down the back to devein. Rinse the heads well and dry on paper towels.

2. Heat the oil in a saucepan, add the shrimp heads and fry until they turn pink. Add the boiling water, garlic, lemon grass if using, chili sauce and lime juice. Bring to the boil, then cover and simmer for 25 minutes. Strain the stock and return to the pan with the lemon juice and salt.

3. Just before serving, add the shrimp and simmer until pink. Stir in half the scallion, chili and cilantro leaves and serve the remainder in a separate bowl to serve.

Serves 4
Preparation time:
20 minutes
Cooking time:
25 minutes
Freezing:
Recommended

WATERCRESS AND CHICKEN SOUP

The success of this soup depends greatly on the quality of the stock, so it is not one where you can cheat with cubes. Japanese soy sauce is also called shoyu, it has a more subtle flavor than Chinese soy sauce.

*¹/₂ lb skinned boneless
   chicken breast
2 tablespoons dry sherry or
   rice wine
5 cups Chicken Stock**

*1 tablespoon Japanese soy
   sauce
1 bunch watercress,
   chopped roughly
salt to taste*

Serves 4
Preparation time:
15 minutes
Cooking time:
8 minutes
Freezing:
Not recommended

1. Slice the chicken into wafer-thin slivers across the grain. Place in a bowl and sprinkle with the sherry or rice wine and a little salt.
2. Bring the stock and soy sauce to the boil. Add the chicken, cover and simmer for 5 minutes. Add the watercress and simmer for 1 minute. Serve immediately.

MINTED PEA SOUP

This soup is a good way of using peas when they are plentiful and cheap. If you use home grown peas, don't discard the pods—wash them and simmer in the stock for 30 minutes, then strain and use as directed below—they improve the flavor of the soup.

*¹/₄ cup butter
2 shallots, chopped
2 celery sticks, chopped
1 tablespoon chopped mint
1 lb fresh peas
4 cups Chicken or
   Vegetable Stock**

*¹/₃ cucumber, peeled and
   diced
¹/₂ romaine, shredded
salt and pepper to taste
mint sprigs to garnish*

Serves 4
Preparation time:
35 minutes
Cooking time:
25 minutes
Freezing:
Not recommended

1. Melt the butter in a large saucepan, add the shallots and celery and fry gently until softened. Stir in the mint and peas and cook for 1 minute.
2. Add the stock, bring to the boil, then cover and simmer for 15 minutes. Add the cucumber, lettuce, and salt and pepper and simmer for 10 minutes.
3. Puree half of the soup in a food processor or blender, then return to the pan. Serve piping hot, garnished with mint sprigs.

SUMMER

MINTED AVOCADO DIP

Avocado flesh discolors quickly, but if you place the pit in the prepared dip and cover with plastic wrap it will stay green for a few hours.

2 ripe avocados
2 tablespoons lemon juice
2 tablespoons plain yogurt
1 clove garlic, crushed
1 tablespoon chopped mint

salt and pepper to taste
TO SERVE:
4–6 pitta breads
mint sprigs

Serves 4
Preparation time:
15 minutes
Freezing:
Not recommended

1. Halve and pit the avocados. Spoon the flesh into a bowl and mash with a fork until soft and smooth.
2. Stir in the remaining ingredients and mix well. Turn into a serving dish or onto 4 individual plates.
3. Broil the pitta breads on both sides and cut into halves or fingers. Garnish the avocado dip with mint sprigs and serve with the warm pitta bread.

LATE SUMMER SALAD

Give yourself plenty of time to prepare and arrange the vegetables for this colorful salad. Serve with lots of freshly ground black pepper.

1 cup finely shredded red
   cabbage
1 ear of corn, cooked and
   sliced into rings
1/3 lb each raw beet and
   zucchini, cut into
   matchstick pieces
1/4 lb mushrooms, sliced
   thinly

2/3 cup shelled beech nuts
2 tablespoons tarragon
   vinegar
1/4 cup filbert or walnut oil
1 tablespoon Greek
   strained yogurt
1 teaspoon Dijon mustard
salt and pepper to taste

Serves 4
Preparation time:
30 minutes
Freezing:
Not recommended

1. Arrange the vegetables in neat piles on 4 individual plates. Sprinkle the nuts over the top.
2. Beat the remaining ingredients together with a fork until thick. Drizzle over the salads just before serving.

MARINATED ARTICHOKES WITH SALAMI

Sprinkle the artichokes with lemon juice as you prepare them to prevent discoloration. When they are not in season—or are too expensive—use a 14 oz can artichoke hearts, well drained and rinsed.

4–6 globe artichokes
¹/₄ cup lemon juice
2 tablespoons olive oil
1 tablespoon chopped
* parsley*

2 teaspoons chopped
* cilantro leaves*
¹/₄ lb salami, sliced thinly
salt and pepper to taste
lemon slices to garnish

Serves 4
Preparation time:
30 minutes, plus chilling
Cooking time:
20–25 minutes
Freezing:
Not recommended

1. Remove the artichoke stalks and peel off the tough outer leaves, until you reach the tender yellow leaves. Cut off and discard the top two-thirds of the leaves, using a stainless steel knife. Peel the base of the artichokes to remove the tough leaf bases. Quarter the artichokes and remove the hairy chokes.
2. Add 3 tablespoons of the lemon juice to a pan of boiling salted water. Add the artichoke hearts and cook for 20–25 minutes, until tender. Drain and cool quickly under cold running water. Drain well, pat dry with paper towels and place in a bowl.
3. Mix together the remaining lemon juice, olive oil, herbs, and salt and pepper. Pour over the artichokes and stir well. Chill for 1–2 hours, if possible.
4. Arrange the salami and artichoke hearts on 4 individual plates and garnish with lemon slices to serve.

ARTICHOKES WITH MARINATED MUSHROOMS AND PARMA HAM

Make this appetizer up to a day in advance if necessary; keep the artichokes and filling separate until serving time.

4 globe artichokes
¹/₃ cup wine vinegar
3 tablespoons lemon juice
¹/₃ cup olive oil
1 tablespoon chopped
* parsley*

2 teaspoons Dijon mustard
¹/₄ lb mushrooms, sliced
* thinly*
2 oz Parma ham, cut into
* thin strips*
salt and pepper to taste

1. Trim the stalks from the artichokes and remove any tough leaves from the base; wash well. Bring a large pan of water to the boil, add the vinegar and artichokes, cover and cook for about 35 minutes, until a leaf can be pulled out easily. Drain upside down in a colander and leave to cool.

2. Beat the lemon juice, oil, parsley, mustard, and salt and pepper together until thick. Place the mushrooms and ham in a small bowl, pour over the dressing and toss well. Leave to marinate for at least 1 hour.

3. Open out the leaves from each artichoke and carefully remove the hairy choke with a teaspoon. Place the artichokes on 4 individual plates and fill the centers with the mushroom mixture.

Serves 4
Preparation time: 30 minutes, plus marinating
Preparation time: About 35 minutes
Freezing: Not recommended

VEGETABLES WITH GREEN SAUCE

This sharp-tasting green sauce provides a lively dip for all
kinds of raw summer vegetables.

*1 1/2–2 lb fresh summer
    vegetables, e.g. zucchini,
    fennel, peppers, carrots,
    cherry tomatoes, lettuce
    hearts, scallions, snow
    peas*
FOR THE SAUCE:
1 clove garlic, crushed

*1 tablespoon capers,
    chopped finely*
*3 tablespoons chopped
    parsley*
1 tablespoon wine vinegar
1 teaspoon Dijon mustard
1/3 cup olive oil
salt and pepper to taste

Serves 4–6
Preparation time:
30 minutes
Freezing:
Not recommended

1. First prepare the sauce. Mix together the garlic, capers,
parsley, vinegar and mustard. Stir in the oil a little at a time,
then season with salt and pepper. Place in a small bowl.
2. Cut the vegetables into large chunks, or whole if small.
Arrange in a large bowl or basket, or on 4–6 individual
plates, and serve with the green sauce for dipping.

CRUDITÉS WITH MUSTARD MAYONNAISE

Adapt the recipe to each season, choosing the freshest,
most colorful vegetables available which offer a variety of
textures and flavors.

*1 red pepper, cored and
    seeded*
2–3 zucchini
2–3 carrots
1/2 cauliflower
1/4 lb mushrooms
1 bunch radishes

1/3 cup mayonnaise
2 teaspoons wine vinegar
1 tablespoon olive oil
*1 teaspoon coarse grain
    mustard*
salt and pepper to taste

Serves 4
Preparation time:
25 minutes
Freezing:
Not recommended

1. Have ready a bowl of ice water if you are preparing the
vegetables in advance. Cut the pepper into strips. Cut the
zucchini and carrots into sticks. Break the cauliflower into
small florets. Place all the vegetables in the ice water if
necessary.
2. Mix the remaining ingredients together and place in a
small bowl set on a large platter.
3. Drain the vegetables thoroughly if necessary and
arrange in piles around the edge of the platter.

PROVENCE-STYLE GREEN BEANS

1 lb green beans
2 tablespoons olive oil
2 cloves garlic, chopped
* finely*

2 tomatoes, skinned and
* chopped*
salt and pepper to taste

1. Cook the beans in boiling salted water for about 10 minutes, until just tender. Drain well and set aside.
2. Heat the oil in a saucepan, add the garlic, and salt and pepper and fry gently for 2 minutes. Add the tomatoes and cook for 2–3 minutes, until they become slightly pulpy. Add the beans, stirring well, cover and cook for 3–4 minutes.
3. Divide between 4 individual warmed plates and serve piping hot, with French bread to mop up the juices.

Serves 4
Preparation time: 15 minutes
Cooking time: About 20 minutes
Freezing: Not recommended

ASPARAGUS WITH CREAM AND ALMONDS

A topping of seasoned cream and sweet almonds pushes this asparagus dish into the sublime!

1 lb asparagus
²/₃ cup heavy cream
1 tablespoon lemon juice

¹/₄ cup slivered almonds,
*   toasted*
salt and pepper to taste

Serves 4
Preparation time:
15 minutes
Cooking time:
12–15 minutes
Freezing:
Not recommended

1. Bend the asparagus spears until they snap. Discard the tough ends (or peel and use to make soup). Boil or steam the asparagus spears for 12–15 minutes, until tender.
2. Whip the cream until fairly stiff. Fold in half of the lemon juice and season with salt and pepper.
3. Arrange the asparagus on 4 individual warmed plates. Sprinkle over the remaining lemon juice, then top with a spoonful of cream. Sprinkle with the almonds and serve immediately.

ASPARAGUS AND EGG TARTS

When asparagus is out of season, use lightly cooked green beans, broccoli or spinach. Use sifted all-purpose flour or whole wheat flour for the pastry, according to taste.

¹/₃ lb shortcrust pastry (see
*   Country Garden Tarts,*
*   page 64)*
¹/₃ lb asparagus, cooked
4 eggs

4 teaspoons whipping
*   cream*
4 teaspoons grated
*   Parmesan cheese*

Serves 4
Preparation time:
20 minutes, plus
making pastry
Cooking time:
30–35 minutes
Freezing:
Not recommended

1. Roll out the pastry on a floured surface and use to line four 4 inch tart cups. Line with waxed paper, fill with baking beans or rice and bake blind in a 400°F oven for 10 minutes. Remove the paper and beans and return to the oven for 5 minutes, until browned. Lower the temperature to 350°F.
2. Curl the asparagus around the inside edge of each tart case. Break an egg into the center of each, then top with a teaspoon each of cream and Parmesan cheese.
3. Return the tarts to the oven for 15–20 minutes, until the egg has just set. Serve warm.

GINGERED SHRIMP

You can cook these shrimp on the barbecue as part of an
outdoor meal.

12 uncooked large shrimp
2 tablespoons sunflower
  oil
3 tablespoons lemon juice
1 onion, grated
2 cloves garlic, crushed

2 teaspoons grated fresh
  root ginger
1/2 teaspoon chili powder
salt and pepper to taste
lemon slices and parsley
  sprigs to garnish

Serves 4
Preparation time:
25 minutes, plus
marinating
Cooking time:
5–6 minutes
Freezing:
Not recommended

1. Peel the shrimp, leaving on the tail ends. Slit along the
back to devein. Thread the shrimp onto 4 bamboo
skewers.
2. Mix together the remaining ingredients, brush all over
the shrimp and leave to marinate for 1 hour, occasionally
brushing with more mixture.
3. Broil the shrimp for 5–6 minutes, turning once, until
they are pink and lightly browned. Garnish with lemon
and parsley to serve.

SASHIMI

Use only perfectly fresh fish for this raw fish dish.

1 salmon steak or salmon
  trout, weighing about
  1/2 lb
1/3 lb firm white fish, e.g.
  bass, turbot, halibut
1/4 lb white radish, grated

1 carrot, grated
1 small turnip, grated
1 tablespoon Japanese
  horseradish
2/3 cup Japanese soy sauce
  (shoyu)

Serves 4
Preparation time:
25–30 minutes,
plus chilling
Freezing:
Not recommended

1. Remove the skin and bones from all fish. Using a very
sharp knife, cut the fish into wafer-thin slices and arrange
attractively on 4 individual plates.
2. Place piles of radish, and carrot and turnip on each
plate, cover and chill for 1 hour.
3. Blend the Japanese horseradish to a smooth paste with
water and place a little on each plate. Divide the soy sauce
between 4 tiny bowls, and place beside the plates.
4. To eat, dip the slivers of fish first into the horseradish,
then the soy sauce.

SMOKED TROUT PUREE WITH FRESH TOMATO SAUCE

Smoked trout can be bought already filleted, or as whole fish. If you buy whole fish you will need nearly 1 lb. Carefully remove the skin and bones before using.

½ lb smoked trout fillets, chopped
1 tablespoon lemon juice
1 teaspoon grated lemon rind
pinch of ground red pepper

⅓ cup Greek strained yogurt
1 teaspoon chopped dill
½ lb ripe tomatoes, skinned and seeded
salt and pepper to taste
dill sprigs to garnish

Serves 4
Preparation time: 25 minutes, plus chilling
Freezing: Recommended

1. Place the trout, lemon juice and rind, ground red pepper, yogurt, dill, and salt and pepper in a blender or food processor and work together until smooth. Place in a bowl and chill for 1 hour.
2. Puree the tomatoes, seasoned with salt and pepper, in the blender or food processor.
3. To serve, place a spoonful of tomato sauce on 4 individual plates. Place spoonfuls of smoked trout puree on top and garnish with dill. Serve with fingers or triangles of whole wheat toast.

SMOKED SALMON WHIRLS

These morsels of smoked salmon wrapped around a creamy filling make an elegant appetizer for a summer meal.

⅓ lb smoked salmon
½ cup curd cheese or farmer's cheese
1 teaspoon lemon juice

2 tablespoons snipped chives
black pepper to taste
mustard and cress or alfalfa sprouts to garnish

Serves 4
Preparation time: 10 minutes, plus chilling
Freezing: Not recommended

1. Place the salmon on a board, overlapping the slices to make 2 roughly 6 × 4 inch rectangles.
2. Beat together the cheese, lemon juice, chives and pepper and spread carefully over the salmon. Roll up each rectangle carefully from one long edge, place on a plate and chill for 1 hour, until firm.
3. Using a sharp knife, cut the rolls into thin slices and arrange in a circle on 4 individual plates. Garnish with little bundles of sprouts.

HERBED YOGURT CHEESE

Plain yogurt makes a delightful fresh soft cheese, perfect for summer days. Start the preparations the day before required.

2 cups plain yogurt
1/2 teaspoon salt
2 tablespoons chopped
  herbs, e.g. chives, parsley,
  basil, oregano, tarragon
pepper to taste

tarragon sprigs to garnish
TO SERVE:
2 tablespoons olive oil
1 clove garlic, crushed
8–12 slices French bread
2 bunches radishes

Serves 4
Preparation time:
20 minutes, plus
draining time
Freezing:
Not recommended

1. Line a sieve with muslin or a clean fine dish cloth and place over a bowl.
2. Mix together the yogurt and salt, pour into the sieve and leave to drain for 12 hours, or overnight.
3. Turn the yogurt cheese into a bowl and mix with the herbs and pepper.
4. Mix together the oil and garlic. Toast the bread on one side. Brush the untoasted side with the garlic oil, then toast until brown and crisp.
5. Garnish the yogurt cheese with tarragon and serve with the radishes and garlic toast.

LETTUCE AND CHERVIL SOUP

1 large romaine, shredded
2 1/2 cups hot Chicken
  Stock*
bunch of chervil
2 1/2 cups milk

pinch of grated nutmeg
1 tablespoon lemon juice
salt and pepper to taste
4–6 thin slices lemon to
  garnish

Serves 4–6
Preparation time:
20 minutes
Cooking time:
15 minutes
Freezing:
Not recommended

1. Place the lettuce, stock, chervil, and salt and pepper in a large pan. Bring to the boil, then cover and simmer for 10 minutes, until the lettuce is tender. Puree in a blender or food processor.
2. Return the soup to the pan, add the milk and nutmeg and heat gently. Check the seasoning.
3. Just before serving, stir in the lemon juice. Pour into individual warmed soup plates and float a slice of lemon on top of each serving.

COUNTRY HERB SOUP

The wonderful flavor of fresh herbs is delightfully refreshing in this stylish summer soup.

2 tablespoons butter
1 large onion, chopped
1 leek, sliced
1 lb spinach, chopped
1 potato, chopped
1 tablespoon each chopped
* parsley, mint and chives*

2 teaspoons chopped thyme
5 cups Vegetable Stock*
²/₃ cup whipping cream
salt and pepper to taste
parsley sprigs to garnish

Serves 4
Preparation time:
25 minutes
Cooking time:
15–20 minutes
Freezing:
Not recommended

1. Melt the butter in a large saucepan, add the onion and leek and fry gently until softened. Add the spinach, potato, herbs and stock. Bring to the boil, then cover and simmer for 15–20 minutes, until the potato is tender.
2. Puree the soup in a blender or food processor. Return to the pan, add the cream, and salt and pepper and reheat gently. Serve hot, garnished with parsley.

WATERCRESS AND LEEK SOUP

To serve chilled, use 2 tablespoons salad oil in place of butter.

2 tablespoons butter
1 leek, sliced thinly
2 bunches watercress,
* chopped*
4 cups hot Vegetable Stock*
strip of orange rind
3 tablespoons freshly
* squeezed orange juice*

2 teaspoons cornstarch,
* blended with 3*
* tablespoons whipping*
* cream*
salt and pepper to taste
shredded orange rind to
* garnish*

Serves 4
Preparation time:
20 minutes
Cooking time:
8–10 minutes
Freezing:
Recommended, at
end of stage 2

1. Melt the butter in a saucepan, add the leek and fry gently until softened. Add the watercress and stir until slightly wilted.
2. Add the hot stock and bring to the boil. Add the orange rind and juice, and salt and pepper, cover and simmer for 5 minutes, then puree in a blender or food processor until fairly smooth.
3. Return the soup to the pan, stir in the blended cornstarch and cook until slightly thickened and smooth.
4. Serve hot or cold, garnished with orange rind and accompanied by Cheese Sticks* or small cheese crackers.

CHILLED TOMATO AND BASIL SOUP

Tomato and basil are natural partners and taste particularly good in this refreshing summer soup. Make it the day before required, if you wish.

1 tablespoon salad oil
1 onion, chopped
1 potato, chopped
1 lb tomatoes, skinned and
  quartered
2 tablespoons tomato paste

10 basil leaves
1¼ cups Vegetable Stock*
⅔ cup plain yogurt
salt and pepper to taste
snipped chives to garnish

Serves 4
Preparation time:
15 minutes, plus
chilling
Cooking time:
20 minutes
Freezing:
Recommended

1. Heat the oil in a pan, add the onion and fry until softened. Add the potato and stir well. Add the tomatoes, tomato paste, basil, stock, and salt and pepper, bring to the boil, then cover and simmer for 20 minutes.
2. Puree the soup in a blender or food processor, then stir in half of the yogurt. Leave to cool, then chill for at least 2 hours.
3. Transfer the soup to 4 individual bowls. Top with a spoonful of the remaining yogurt and a sprinkling of snipped chives to serve.

CHILLED CATALAN SOUP

This soup is similar to gazpacho, but with less tomato and more green vegetables. Ground almonds are added to thicken the soup slightly and add to the flavors.

1 Spanish onion, chopped
1 green pepper, cored, seeded and chopped
2 cloves garlic, crushed
1/2 cucumber, chopped
1/2 lb ripe tomatoes, skinned and chopped
1/4 cup ground almonds
1 tablespoon chopped parsley

2 tablespoons chopped mint
2 tablespoons olive oil
3 tablespoons wine vinegar
2 1/2 cups water
salt and pepper to taste
TO SERVE:
ice cubes
stuffed olives, sliced

1. Place all the ingredients, except the water, and salt and pepper, in a blender or food processor and work together until finely chopped. Add the water, and salt and pepper and process again. Transfer to a bowl, cover and chill for 2–3 hours.
2. Serve in individual bowls with a few ice cubes and olive slices on top.

Serves 4
Preparation time: 30 minutes, plus chilling
Freezing: Not recommended

FALL

ITALIAN BAKED TOMATOES

4 beefsteak tomatoes
1/2 cup breadcrumbs,
   toasted
1 tablespoon chopped
   mixed herbs, e.g.
   tarragon, mint, chives
   and parsley

1/4 lb mushrooms, chopped
1/3 cup grated Parmesan
   cheese
salt and pepper to taste
curly endive and parsley
   sprigs to garnish

Serves 4
Preparation time:
20 minutes
Cooking time:
15 minutes
Freezing:
Not recommended

1. Cut the tops off the tomatoes and scoop out the flesh into a sieve placed over a bowl. Sprinkle the insides of the tomatoes with salt and place upside down.
2. Press the tomato flesh through the sieve. Stir in the breadcrumbs, herbs, mushrooms, and salt and pepper.
3. Place the tomatoes in an oiled baking dish, fill with the mushroom mixture and sprinkle with the cheese. Bake in a 375°F oven for 15 minutes, until the tomatoes are tender. Serve warm or cold, garnished with curly endive and parsley.

GARLIC-BAKED PEPPERS WITH OLIVES

Try to get three different colored peppers if possible as they look stunning on the plate. The peppers are baked for a short time to bring out their sweet flavor while keeping their delicious crunchy texture.

1 each red, green and
   yellow pepper,
   quartered, cored and
   seeded
2 cloves garlic, chopped
   finely

2 tomatoes, skinned and
   chopped finely
1 teaspoon capers, chopped
12 black olives
2 tablespoons olive oil
salt and pepper to taste

Serves 4
Preparation time:
15 minutes
Cooking time:
25 minutes
Freezing:
Not recommended

1. Place the peppers skin side down in a greased baking dish. Mix together the garlic, tomatoes, capers, and salt and pepper and spoon a little into each pepper quarter. Top each with an olive and drizzle over the oil.
2. Bake in a 375°F oven for 25 minutes. Serve warm or cold.

CELERIAC WITH EGG AND TARRAGON DRESSING

*1 celeriac, weighing about
    1 lb
1 tablespoon lemon juice
2 egg yolks
1 tablespoon tarragon
    vinegar*

*1 tablespoon Dijon
    mustard
2 tablespoons olive oil
2 tablespoons sour cream
salt and pepper to taste
2 teaspoons chopped
    tarragon to garnish*

Serves 4
Preparation time:
20 minutes
Freezing:
Not recommended

1. Peel the celeriac thickly. Slice it thinly, then cut each slice into matchstick pieces. Place in a bowl with the lemon juice and mix well.
2. Beat together the egg yolks, vinegar, mustard, and salt and pepper, then gradually add the oil and sour cream. Add to the celeriac and mix well.
3. Pile the celeriac onto 4 individual plates and sprinkle with chopped tarragon. Serve as soon as possible.

EGGPLANT AND TAHINI PUREE

Tahini is ground sesame paste. It has a warm subtle flavor which goes well with lightly spiced eggplant.

*1 lb eggplant
1 clove garlic
1 teaspoon salt
3 tablespoons tahini
$^{1}/_{3}$ cup lemon juice
$^{1}/_{2}$ teaspoon chili powder
1 teaspoon ground cumin*

*TO SERVE:
1 tablespoon olive oil
1 tablespoon chopped
    parsley
few black olives
pitta bread
lemon wedges*

Serves 4
Preparation time:
10 minutes, plus
cooling
Cooking time:
25–30 minutes
Freezing:
Recommended

1. Make 3 long slits in the eggplant, place on a baking sheet and bake in a 425°F oven for 25–30 minutes, until the flesh feels soft. Leave until cool enough to handle.
2. Cut the eggplant in half and scoop out the flesh. Place in a blender or food processor with the garlic and salt and work together until smooth. Add the remaining ingredients and blend well. Transfer to a small bowl and leave to cool.
3. Just before serving, drizzle over the oil, sprinkle with the parsley and top with a few olives. Serve with triangles of warm pitta bread and lemon wedges.

PAKORAS WITH MINT CHUTNEY

Pakora batter is usually made with garbanzo bean flour, which is very hard to find. Semolina works equally well and gives the fritters the same golden color.

²/₃ cup semolina
1 teaspoon salt
¹/₂ teaspoon chili powder
1 teaspoon turmeric
1 teaspoon garam masala
2 tablespoons plain yogurt
³/₄ cup water
1 lb vegetables, e.g.
*   cauliflower, eggplant,*
*   zucchini, peppers,*
*   mushrooms*

salad oil for deep-frying
mint sprigs to garnish
FOR THE CHUTNEY:
¹/₃ cup chopped mint
1 small onion, chopped
*   finely*
1 teaspoon chili powder
¹/₄ cup plain yogurt
2 teaspoons honey
2 tablespoons vinegar
salt and pepper to taste

Serves 4
Preparation time:
30 minutes, plus
standing time
Cooking time:
2–3 minutes per
batch
Freezing:
Not recommended

1. Mix together the semolina, salt and spices in a bowl. Make a well in the center and add the yogurt. Beat with a wooden spoon, gradually adding the water, to make a smooth batter. Leave to rest for 10 minutes.
2. Mix together the chutney ingredients and place in a small bowl. Cover and chill until required.
3. Prepare the vegetables; break the cauliflower into small florets, dice the eggplant, slice the zucchini, cut the peppers into strips; slice the mushrooms if large or leave whole if small. Add to the batter and stir to coat well.
4. Heat the oil in a large saucepan and deep-fry the vegetables in batches for 2–3 minutes, until crisp and golden. Drain well on paper towels, and keep warm.
5. Garnish the pakoras with mint sprigs and serve hot with the chutney as a dipping sauce.

HOT GARLIC MUSHROOMS

These delicious mushrooms can be prepared in advance, ready to go in the oven.

4 small slices whole wheat
*   bread*
¹/₄ cup butter
1 clove garlic, crushed

1 lb mushrooms, stalks
*   removed*
4 teaspoons lemon juice
salt and pepper to taste

1. Butter 4 ramekins or other small ovenproof dishes. Cut the bread into circles the same diameter as the dishes.

2. Beat together the butter, garlic, and salt and pepper. Spread a little on each slice of bread and place buttered side up in the dishes.

3. Pile the mushrooms into the dishes and spread the remaining garlic butter on top. Sprinkle with the lemon juice, and salt and pepper.

4. Cover with foil and bake in a 425°F oven for 25 minutes, until tender. Serve piping hot.

Serves 4
Preparation time:
15 minutes
Cooking time:
25 minutes
Freezing:
Not recommended

TAGLIATELLE WITH PECAN AND PARSLEY SAUCE

Use a mixture of green and white tagliatelle, if possible.

1/2 cup shelled pecans
1/2 cup parsley
2 tablespoons butter,
* softened*
3 tablespoons grated
* Parmesan cheese*

2/3 cup olive oil
2 tablespoons cream cheese
* whipped with 1 1/2*
* teaspoons lemon juice*
3/4 lb fresh tagliatelle or
* noodles*
salt and pepper to taste

Serves 4
Preparation time:
20 minutes
Cooking time:
6–8 minutes
Freezing:
Not recommended

1. Place two-thirds of the pecans and the parsley in a food processor or blender and work together until finely ground. Add the butter and Parmesan cheese and blend to mix well. Add the oil, a little at a time, and blend until the sauce is smooth and thick. Stir in the cream cheese mixture and season with salt and pepper.
2. Cook the tagliatelle according to package instructions. Drain well, then return to the pan with the sauce and heat gently, stirring to mix.
3. Transfer to 4 warmed individual plates. Roughly chop the remaining pecans and sprinkle over the pasta. Serve immediately.

GREEN GNOCCHI WITH TOMATO SAUCE

If you like, the gnocchi can be prepared, but not cooked, well in advance, and the sauce made ready for reheating.

1 lb spinach
2 tablespoons butter or
* margarine*
1 shallot, chopped finely
1/2 cup curd cheese or
* farmer's cheese*
2 egg yolks
3/4 cup all-purpose flour
2/3 cup grated Parmesan
* cheese*

grated nutmeg
salt and pepper to taste
FOR THE SAUCE:
3/4 lb ripe tomatoes,
* skinned and chopped*
1 tablespoon tomato paste
pinch of sugar
2 tablespoons heavy cream

1. Place the spinach, with just the water clinging to the leaves after washing, in a large pan and cook for about 5 minutes, until tender. Drain well, pressing out as much water as possible, then chop finely. Place in a bowl.

2. Melt the butter or margarine in a small pan, add the shallot and fry until softened. Add to the spinach with the curd cheese, and salt and pepper. Mix well, then work in the egg yolks, flour, Parmesan cheese and a sprinkling of nutmeg. Cover and chill for at least 30 minutes, until firm.

3. Meanwhile, prepare the sauce. Place the tomatoes, tomato paste and sugar in a small pan. Heat gently until the tomatoes become more liquid, bring to the boil, then simmer for 10 minutes. Press through a sieve, return to the pan, add the cream and heat gently while cooking the gnocchi.

4. Have ready a pan of salted simmering water. Shape the gnocchi into ¾ inch balls. Add half to the pan and cook for about 5 minutes, or until they rise to the surface of the water. Remove with a slotted spoon and keep warm while you cook the rest.

5. Divide the gnocchi between 4 individual warmed dishes and pour over the tomato sauce to serve.

Serves 4
Preparation time:
45 minutes, plus chilling
Cooking time:
About 5 minutes per batch
Freezing:
Not recommended

CHICKEN LIVER AND SAGE CROSTINI

2 tablespoons olive oil
1 shallot, chopped
1 clove garlic, crushed
¹/₂ lb chicken livers,
   chopped
1 cup halved mushrooms
8 small sage leaves

¹/₄ cup dry white wine
salt and pepper to taste
TO SERVE:
4 slices French bread, cut
   diagonally, fried in
   salad oil
sage leaves to garnish

Serves 4
Preparation time:
15 minutes
Cooking time:
10 minutes
Freezing:
Not recommended

1. Heat the oil in a frying pan, add the shallot and garlic and fry until softened.
2. Increase the heat, add the chicken livers and cook, stirring, until evenly colored. Stir in the mushrooms and sage and cook for 1 minute.
3. Add the wine, and salt and pepper and cook for 2–3 minutes, until the livers are cooked but still pink inside.
4. Arrange the fried bread on 4 warmed individual plates, pile the chicken liver mixture on top and garnish with the sage leaves. Serve hot.

BROILED GREEK CHEESE PARCELS

A simple appetizer, but one which is sure to be a great success—the slightly sharp tasting vine leaves go so well with the creamy melting cheese.

¹/₂ lb package vine leaves
3 cups Feta cheese, cut into
   small squares

TO SERVE:
few vine leaves (optional)
lemon slices

Serves 4
Preparation time:
10 minutes, plus
soaking time
Cooking time:
5 minutes
Freezing:
Not recommended

1. Separate the vine leaves and place in a bowl. Pour over boiling water and leave to soak for 20 minutes. Drain and place in a bowl with cold water to cover for 10 minutes. Drain well and dry with paper towels.
2. Wrap each piece of cheese in a vine leaf, securing with wooden cocktail sticks if necessary. Broil for 5 minutes, until the cheese has melted.
3. Remove the cocktail sticks, if used, and serve the parcels on vine leaves if you wish, garnished with lemon slices.

SEASHELLS

1 cup sifted all-purpose
  flour
1 teaspoon dry mustard
$^{1}/_{2}$ cup grated Cheddar
  cheese
$^{1}/_{4}$ cup butter or margarine
1 tablespoon water
$^{1}/_{4}$ lb shelled medium-size
  shrimp (thawed if
  frozen)

$^{1}/_{4}$ lb fresh or canned crab
  meat, drained and
  flaked
1 egg, beaten
$^{2}/_{3}$ cup whipping cream
1 tablespoon snipped
  chives
salt and pepper to taste
parsley sprigs to garnish

Serves 4
Preparation time:
20 minutes
Cooking time:
30–35 minutes
Freezing:
Recommended

1. Mix together the flour, mustard, half of the cheese, and salt and pepper. Rub in the butter or margarine until the mixture resembles breadcrumbs. Stir in the water and mix to a firm dough. Knead lightly.
2. Divide the dough into 4 pieces, then roll out to line 4 scallop shells. Trim the edges and prick the base.
3. Bake in a 400°F oven for 15 minutes, until golden brown. Lower the temperature to 350°F.
4. Fill the pastry cases with the shrimp and crab. Beat together the egg, cream, chives, and salt and pepper. Pour into the shells and sprinkle with the remaining cheese. Return to the oven for 15–20 minutes, until the filling is just firm. Serve hot, garnished with parsley.

HOT BROILED AVOCADO

2 large ripe avocados,
  halved and pitted
$^{1}/_{3}$ lb fresh or canned crab
  meat, drained
3 tablespoons whipping
  cream

$^{1}/_{2}$ teaspoon paprika
2 tablespoons whole wheat
  breadcrumbs
$^{1}/_{2}$ cup grated Gruyère
  cheese
salt to taste

Serves 4
Preparation time:
10–15 minutes
Cooking time:
3–4 minutes
Freezing:
Not recommended

1. Place the avocados cut side up in an ovenproof dish. Mix together the crab, cream, paprika and a little salt, then pile into the avocados.
2. Mix together the breadcrumbs and cheese and sprinkle over the avocados. Broil for 3–4 minutes, until the topping is crisp and golden brown. Serve immediately.

SMOKED HADDOCK SOUP

This soup is a slight variation of a traditional Scottish one called Cullen Skink. I sometimes add a few peas or skinned and chopped tomatoes for extra color.

1 lb smoked haddock
2¹/₂ cups milk
1¹/₄ cups water
2 tablespoons butter
1 tablespoon salad oil
1 onion, chopped finely

³/₄ lb floury potatoes, diced
2 tablespoons chopped
*   parsley*
grated nutmeg and pepper
*   to taste*

Serves 4
Preparation time: 30 minutes
Cooking time: About 20 minutes
Freezing: Recommended

1. Place the haddock, milk and water in a saucepan, bring to the boil, then cover and simmer for 10 minutes, until the fish flakes easily. Carefully transfer with a spatula to a plate and leave to cool slightly. Strain the cooking liquid and set aside.
2. Heat the butter and oil in the saucepan, add the onion and fry until softened. Add the potatoes and cook for 5 minutes. Add the reserved cooking liquid, bring to the boil, then cover and simmer for about 20 minutes, until the potato has broken down; mash it if necessary.
3. Skin and flake the fish and add to the soup with the nutmeg, pepper and parsley. Heat gently for 5 minutes. Serve with whole wheat bread.

LEMON SOLE BAKED IN A PAPER CASE

Allow everyone to open their own parcel—the aroma that escapes is almost as good as the taste.

1 small fennel
1 tablespoon salad oil
1 shallot, chopped
1 leek, shredded

4 tomatoes, skinned,
*   seeded and chopped*
4 lemon sole fillets, each
*   weighing about ¹/₄ lb*
salt and pepper to taste

1. Remove the feathery leaves from the fennel and reserve. Cut the fennel into fine julienne strips.
2. Heat the oil in a small pan, add the shallot and fry over high heat for 1 minute. Lower the heat, add the leek and fennel and fry for 5 minutes. Add the tomatoes, and salt and pepper and simmer for 5 minutes.
3. Cut out 4 heart-shaped pieces of waxed paper, twice the size of the fish, and brush with oil. Place the fish on one

half, spoon over the sauce and sprinkle with the reserved fennel leaves. Fold the paper over to enclose the fish and seal well.

4. Place the parcels on 2 baking sheets and bake in a 400°F oven for 10 minutes. Serve the fish in the unopened parcels, placed on individual warmed plates.

Serves 4
Preparation time:
35 minutes
Cooking time:
10 minutes
Freezing:
Not recommended

STILTON, CELERY AND APPLE SOUP

2 tablespoons butter or
   margarine
1 onion, chopped finely
3 celery sticks, chopped
   finely
1 tablespoon all-purpose
   flour
²/₃ cup dry white wine
2¹/₂ cups Vegetable Stock*

1¹/₄ cups milk
1 bay leaf
1 cooking apple, peeled
   and chopped
3 oz Stilton or Danish Blue
   cheese
salt and pepper to taste
celery leaves to garnish

Serves 4
Preparation time:
25 minutes
Cooking time:
30 minutes
Freezing:
Recommended, at
end of stage 2

1. Melt the butter or margarine in a large pan, add the onion and celery and fry gently until slightly softened. Stir in the flour and cook for 1 minute.
2. Gradually stir in the wine and stock and cook, stirring, until thickened and smooth. Add the milk, bay leaf, apple, and salt and pepper. Bring to the boil, then cover and simmer for 30 minutes.
3. Remove from the heat and discard the bay leaf. Crumble in the Stilton or Danish Blue and stir until completely melted. Serve piping hot, garnished with celery leaves.

PUMPKIN SOUP

Pumpkin is usually inexpensive and plentiful in the fall. It makes one of my favorite seasonal soups—rich, creamy and full of flavor.

2 tablespoons olive oil
1 large onion, chopped
1 clove garlic, crushed
¹/₄ lb bacon, chopped
2 lb pumpkin, peeled,
   seeded and chopped
   finely

1 potato, chopped finely
1 bouquet garni
4 cups Vegetable Stock*
1 lb can white kidney
   beans, drained
salt and pepper to taste

Serves 4–6
Preparation time:
35 minutes
Cooking time:
1 hour 10 minutes
Freezing:
Recommended

1. Heat the oil in a large saucepan, add the onion and garlic and fry until softened. Add the bacon and fry for 5 minutes.
2. Add the pumpkin, potato, bouquet garni, stock, and salt and pepper. Bring to the boil, then cover and simmer for 1 hour, until the vegetables are very tender.
3. Stir in the beans and simmer for 10 minutes. Serve hot.

INDONESIAN CHICKEN SOUP

Even those who don't usually like spicy foods will enjoy
this light, sweet-tasting soup.

*1/4 lb boneless chicken
    breast, skinned and
    sliced thinly
1/2 teaspoon turmeric
1/2 teaspoon chili powder
1 tablespoon sunflower oil
3 tablespoons chopped
    scallions
1 cup unsweetened flaked
    coconut, blended with
    2 1/2 cups boiling water
1 1/4 cups Chicken Stock**

*2 tablespoons lime juice
1 teaspoon light brown
    sugar
1/3 cup long-grain rice
1 tablespoon crunchy
    peanut butter
3 oz canned
    waterchestnuts, sliced
    thinly
salt and pepper to taste
chopped scallion tops to
    garnish*

Serves 4
Preparation time:
20 minutes
Cooking time:
12–15 minutes
Freezing:
Recommended

1. Place the chicken, turmeric and chili powder in a bowl
and mix well.
2. Heat the oil in a large saucepan, add the chicken and
stir-fry quickly for about 2 minutes, until browned. Stir in
the scallions.
3. Add the blended coconut, stock, lime juice, sugar, rice
and peanut butter. Bring to the boil, then cover and
simmer for 12–15 minutes, until the rice is cooked.
4. Add the waterchestnuts, and salt and pepper and heat
gently. Pour into 4 individual warmed soup bowls and
sprinkle with chopped scallion tops to serve.

RED ONION SOUP

This soup is similar to the well-loved French onion. The
red onions give it a particularly good flavor and color.

*2 tablespoons butter
1 tablespoon salad oil
1 lb red onions, sliced
    thinly
1/2 teaspoon sugar
2 × 11 oz cans
    concentrated consommé
2 tablespoons sherry*

*pepper to taste
TO SERVE:
4 small slices whole wheat
    bread, toasted
4 teaspoons coarse grain
    mustard
1/4 cup grated Gruyère
    cheese*

1. Melt the butter and oil in a large saucepan, add the onions and fry gently until softened. Add the sugar and cook for 10 minutes.

2. Add the consommé with 2 cans of water, bring to the boil, then cover and simmer for 30 minutes. Add the sherry and simmer for 5 minutes. Season with pepper.

3. Spread the toast with the mustard, cut each slice into quarters and place in 4 individual warmed soup bowls, mustard side up. Pour over the soup and sprinkle with the cheese to serve.

Serves 4
Preparation time:
25 minutes
Cooking time:
45 minutes
Freezing:
Not recommended

FRIED POTATO SKINS

For a casual party, these crispy slivers can be handed around with the drinks. They are great for working up an appetite. Use the potatoes for another dish.

3 lb baking potatoes
²/₃ cup sour cream
1 teaspoon paprika

salad oil for deep-frying
sea salt and pepper to taste

Serves 4
Preparation time:
15 minutes
Cooking time:
3–4 minutes per batch
Freezing:
Not recommended

1. Peel the potatoes into strips, taking a little potato with the skin. Pat dry with paper towels.
2. Mix together the sour cream, paprika and pepper and place in a small dish.
3. Heat the oil to 350°F, or until a potato skin rises instantly to the surface when added. Fry the skins in two batches, until crisp and golden. Drain on paper towels. Sprinkle with sea salt and serve with the sauce for dipping.

STUFFED MUSHROOMS

³/₄ lb flat mushrooms
2 tablespoons salad oil
2 shallots, chopped
1 clove garlic, crushed
¹/₄ lb bacon, chopped finely
1 teaspoon chopped rosemary

¹/₄ cup finely chopped walnuts
1 cup whole wheat breadcrumbs
¹/₂ cup grated Cheddar cheese
salt and pepper to taste

Serves 4
Preparation time:
30 minutes
Cooking time:
10–12 minutes
Freezing:
Not recommended

1. Remove the mushroom stalks and chop finely. Place the mushrooms, open side up, in a large oiled pan.
2. Heat the oil in a frying pan, add the shallots and garlic and fry until softened. Add the bacon and mushroom stalks and fry for 5 minutes.
3. Stir in the rosemary, walnuts, breadcrumbs, and salt and pepper and mix well. Pile a little of the mixture onto each mushroom, then sprinkle with the cheese.
4. Bake in a 400°F oven for 10–12 minutes, until the mushrooms are tender and the cheese has melted. Serve immediately.

STEAMED LEEK PARCELS

These light vegetable parcels with their creamy leek sauce are an ideal way to start a more substantial winter meal, such as a roast or hearty stew.

2 large leeks
3 carrots
3 celery sticks
2 tablespoons butter

1 teaspoon chopped mint
1¼ cups whipping cream
salt and pepper to taste

Serves 4
Preparation time:
30 minutes
Cooking time:
20 minutes
Freezing:
Not recommended

1. Trim the leeks, then cut in half lengthways. Set aside 8 outside strips and finely chop the rest.
2. Cut the carrots and celery into matchstick pieces, about 2½ inches long. Make 8 bundles of carrot and celery sticks and wrap a strip of leek around each. Secure with wooden cocktail sticks.
3. Place the parcels on a heatproof plate with 1 tablespoon water. Cover tightly with foil, place over a pan of simmering water and steam for 20 minutes, until the vegetables are just tender.
4. Meanwile, melt the butter in a small pan, add the chopped leeks and stir well. Cover and cook gently for 2–3 minutes. Add the mint, and salt and pepper and cook for 2 minutes. Stir in the cream, bring gently to simmering point and cook for 2–3 minutes. Puree in a blender or food processor, then return to the pan to keep warm.
5. Spread a pool of leek sauce on 4 individual warmed plates. Remove the cocktail sticks from the vegetables and place 2 parcels on each plate. Serve piping hot.

LENTIL-STUFFED VINE LEAVES

½ lb package vine leaves
in brine, drained
1 small onion, chopped
finely
½ cup red lentils
1¼ cups water
½ teaspoon chili powder
1 teaspoon garam masala
2 teaspoons tomato paste

3 tablespoons raisins
3 tablespoons lemon juice
salt and pepper to taste
TO SERVE:
1 cup Greek strained
yogurt
1 clove garlic, crushed
1–2 tablespoons lemon
juice

1. Place the vine leaves in a bowl, cover with boiling water and leave for 20 minutes. Drain, cover with cold water, leave for another 20 minutes, then drain well.

2. Meanwhile place the onion, lentils, water, chili powder, garam masala, tomato paste, raisins and 1 tablespoon of the lemon juice in a pan. Bring to the boil, then cover tightly and cook gently for about 20 minutes, until all the water is absorbed and the lentils are softened. Season with salt and pepper and leave to cool.

3. Place a teaspoonful of the mixture on each vine leaf and roll up like a parcel, tucking in the ends to enclose the filling completely.

4. Place the parcels in a large frying pan. Add the remaining lemon juice and 1¼ cups water. Bring to the boil, cover tightly and simmer for 30 minutes. Drain.

5. Serve warm or cold with the yogurt, flavored with the garlic and lemon juice.

Serves 6–8
Preparation time: 40 minutes, plus soaking time
Cooking time: 30 minutes
Freezing: Recommended

COUNTRY GARDEN TARTS

Vegetarians in particular should enjoy these little whole wheat tarts packed with crisp vegetables. The cheese can be replaced with vegetarian Cheddar.

FOR THE SHORTCRUST PASTRY:
1¹/₂ cups whole wheat flour
pinch of salt
¹/₃ cup butter or margarine, diced
2 tablespoons water (approximately)
FOR THE FILLING:
2 tablespoons salad oil
1 celery stick, chopped finely
1 leek, sliced thinly

¹/₄ lb broccoli, cut into tiny florets
1 carrot, grated
1 egg
²/₃ cup plain yogurt
¹/₂ cup grated Cheddar cheese
1 tablespoon chopped parsley
salt and pepper to taste
TO SERVE:
curly endive
thinly sliced leek

Serves 4
Preparation time: 40 minutes, plus chilling
Cooking time: 20 minutes
Freezing: Recommended

1. To make the pastry, place the flour and salt in a large bowl and rub in the butter or margarine until the mixture resembles breadcrumbs. Mix in enough water to form a stiff dough.

2. Place on a lightly floured board and knead lightly until smooth. Wrap in foil and chill for 15 minutes.

3. Roll out on a lightly floured board, and use to line four 4 inch tart pans. Line with waxed paper, fill with baking beans or rice and bake blind in a 400°F oven for 10 minutes. Remove the beans and paper and return to the oven for 5 minutes. Lower the temperature to 350°F.

4. Meanwhile, prepare the filling. Heat the oil in a pan, add the celery, leek and broccoli and stir well. Lower the heat, cover the pan and allow the vegetables to sweat for 5 minutes. Add the carrot, and salt and pepper and cook for 5 minutes. Divide between the pastry cases.

5. Beat together the egg, yogurt, cheese, parsley, and salt and pepper, then pour over the vegetables. Return to the oven for 20 minutes, until the filling is firm and golden brown.

6. Carefully remove the tarts from the pans and place on individual plates, lined with curly endive and a few leek rings. Serve warm.

SKEWERED SCALLOPS WITH BACON

When medium-size scallops are not available, use the larger ones and cut into 2 or 3 pieces.

³/₄ lb medium-size scallops
2 tablespoons lime juice
1 tablespoon sunflower oil
1 teaspoon dried dill

¹/₄ lb sliced bacon
salt and pepper to taste
lime wedges and parsley
*   sprigs to serve*

Serves 4
Preparation time:
20 minutes, plus
marinating
Cooking time:
6–8 minutes
Freezing:
Not recommended

1. Place the scallops, lime juice, oil, dill, and salt and pepper in a bowl, mix well, then leave to marinate for 1 hour, stirring occasionally.
2. Stretch the bacon with the back of a knife, then cut each strip into 3 pieces. Wrap each piece around a scallop and thread onto 4 or 8 bamboo skewers.
3. Broil for 6–8 minutes, turning once, until the bacon is crisp and the scallops are cooked. Serve hot, garnished with lime wedges and parsley sprigs.

BAKED MUSSELS

Keep a can of ready-cooked mussels in the pantry to make this speedy appetizer when you're caught unprepared.

¹/₄ cup butter
1 clove garlic, crushed
1 tablespoon chopped
*   parsley*
2 teaspoons lemon juice

¹/₂ lb cooked mussels
¹/₄ lb ready-made puff
*   pastry*
pepper to taste
beaten egg to glaze

Serves 4
Preparation time:
15 minutes
Cooking time:
10–12 minutes
Freezing:
Not recommended

1. Beat together the butter, garlic, parsley, lemon juice and pepper. Divide the mussels between 4 ramekin dishes and spread the garlic butter over the top.
2. Roll out the pastry on a lightly floured surface and cut into 4 circles slightly larger than the ramekins. Dampen the edges of the dishes, press the pastry on top and make a hole in the center. Brush with beaten egg.
3. Bake in a 425°F oven for 10–12 minutes, until the pastry is risen and golden brown. Serve piping hot.

WARM CHICKEN LIVER SALAD

selection of salad leaves,
   e.g. curly endive,
   radicchio, lettuce,
   watercresss
2 tablespoons salad oil
1 shallot, sliced

$^1/_2$ lb chicken livers, halved
$^1/_4$ lb mushrooms, sliced
2 tablespoons red wine
   vinegar
salt and pepper to taste

Serves 4
Preparation time:
15 minutes
Cooking time:
10–15 minutes
Freezing:
Not recommended

1. Tear the leaves into small pieces and arrange on 4 individual plates.
2. Heat the oil in a frying pan, add the shallot and fry until softened. Add the livers and fry quickly for about 5 minutes, until browned all over. Stir in the mushrooms and cook briefly, until just beginning to soften.
3. Remove from the pan with a slotted spoon and divide between the plates of salad.
4. Add the vinegar, and salt and pepper to the pan, stirring to scrape up any pan juices. Bring to the boil, then quickly pour over the chicken livers. Serve immediately.

CHICKEN LIVER AND MUSHROOM PATÉ

$^1/_2$ lb chicken livers
$^1/_4$ cup butter
1 clove garlic, crushed
$^1/_4$ lb mushrooms, chopped
1 tablespoon sherry

1 teaspoon chopped thyme
1 tablespoon each chopped
   parsley and chives
salt and pepper to taste

Serves 4
Preparation time:
15 minutes, plus
chilling
Cooking time:
10 minutes
Freezing:
Recommended

1. Trim off any dark patches from the chicken livers. Rinse and pat dry with paper towels.
2. Melt half of the butter in a frying pan, add the garlic and chicken livers and fry quickly on all sides for about 5 minutes, until evenly browned. Add the mushrooms, sherry, thyme, and salt and pepper and cook gently for 5 minutes.
3. Place in a blender or food processor and work until smooth. Transfer to a small dish, level the top and sprinkle with the parsley and chives.
4. Melt the remaining butter and pour evenly over the top. Leave until set, then chill for 1–2 hours until firm.
5. Remove from the refrigerator 30 minutes before required. Serve with fingers of whole wheat toast and a few salad leaves.

BARBECUED RIBS

2 lb spare ribs
¹/₄ cup honey
3 tablespoons orange juice
3 tablespoons tomato
   catsup

2 teaspoons mustard
3 tablespoons soy sauce
3 tablespoons wine
   vinegar
lemon slices to garnish

1. Arrange the ribs in a single layer on a baking sheet and broil for 12–15 minutes, turning once, until lightly browned and crisp. Drain on paper towels and place in a roasting pan.

2. Mix the remaining ingredients together until smooth, pour over the ribs and mix until well coated.

3. Bake in a 375°F oven for 30-35 minutes, turning occasionally, until tender. Serve piping hot, garnished with lemon slices.

Serves 4
Preparation time: 25 minutes
Cooking time: 30–35 minutes
Freezing: Recommended

BAKED GOATS' CHEESE WITH SALAD

¹/₂ lb chèvre (goats' cheese),
   cut into 4 slices
olive oil for brushing
¹/₂ cup whole wheat
   breadcrumbs
2 teaspoons chopped sage
2 teaspoons snipped chives
FOR THE SALAD:
selection of salad leaves,
   e.g. oak leaf lettuce,
   curly endive, mâche,
   radicchio

6 radishes, sliced
1 cup sliced mushrooms
FOR THE DRESSING:
1 tablespoon lemon juice
3 tablespoons olive oil
¹/₂ teaspoon honey
1 teaspoon Dijon mustard
salt and pepper to taste

Serves 4
Preparation time:
20 minutes
Cooking time:
12–15 minutes
Freezing:
Not recommended

1. Halve each slice of goats' cheese and brush all over with olive oil. Mix together the breadcrumbs, sage and chives and press onto the cheese.

2. Place on a greased baking sheet and bake in a 400°F oven for 12–15 minutes, until the cheese has melted and the coating is crisp.

3. Meanwhile, prepare the salad. Divide the leaves between 4 individual dishes and sprinkle with the radishes and mushrooms.

4. Place the dressing ingredients in a screw-top jar and shake well to mix.

5. Place 2 pieces of hot goats' cheese on top of each salad and pour over the dressing. Serve immediately.

CAMEMBERT PUFF PIE WITH CRANBERRY AND PORT RELISH

Warm creamy Camembert in a crisp crust, served with a tangy cranberry sauce, provides a deliciously different winter appetizer. Use fresh or frozen cranberries.

7 oz ready-made puff
   pastry
9 oz whole Camembert
2 teaspoons green
   peppercorns, crushed
   lightly
beaten egg to glaze
FOR THE RELISH:
1 cup cranberries

2 tablespoons freshly
   squeezed orange juice
¹/₂ teaspoon grated orange
   rind
¹/₃ cup water
¹/₄ cup light brown sugar,
   packed
1 tablespoon port

1. Roll out half of the pastry to a circle slightly larger than the Camembert. Place the Camembert in the center and sprinkle with the peppercorns. Brush the edge of the pastry with beaten egg.

2. Roll out the remaining pastry to a circle large enough to cover the cheese. Place over the cheese, press the edges together to seal, then flute.

3. Place on a baking sheet, brush the top with beaten egg, then slash in a lattice design, taking care not to cut right through the pastry. Bake in a 425°F oven for 15 minutes, until crisp and golden brown.

4. Meanwhile, make the relish. Place all the ingredients in a small pan, bring gently to the boil, then cover and simmer for about 10 minutes, until the cranberries are tender.

5. Cut the pie into 4 wedges and serve immediately, with the warm relish.

Serves 4
Preparation time:
20 minutes
Cooking time:
15 minutes
Freezing:
Not recommended

SPICED PARSNIP SOUP

If the parsnips are large, discard their woody cores.

2 tablespoons butter
1 tablespoon salad oil
1 lb parsnips, chopped
1 onion, chopped
1 teaspoon each ground
  cumin and coriander
2 teaspoons concentrated
  curry paste

1 tablespoon all-purpose
  flour
*2½ cups Chicken Stock**
2 cups milk
⅔ cup whipping cream
salt and pepper to taste
1 carrot, grated, to garnish

Serves 4
Preparation time:
15 minutes
Cooking time:
30 minutes
Freezing:
Not recommended

1. Heat the butter and oil in a large saucepan, add the parsnips and onion and stir well. Lower the heat, cover the pan and allow the vegetables to sweat for 5 minutes.
2. Stir in the cumin, coriander, curry paste and flour and cook for 1 minute, stirring well. Gradually stir in the stock and milk and bring to the boil. Season well with salt and pepper, then cover and simmer for 20 minutes, until the parsnips are tender.
3. Puree in a blender or food processor, return to the pan, add the cream and reheat gently. Divide the soup between 4 individual warmed bowls, add a little pile of grated carrot to each and sprinkle with black pepper.

POTATO AND GARLIC SOUP

Use baking potatoes for this recipe to ensure a smooth creamy texture. Despite the amount of garlic the flavor is quite subtle. Serve with Croutons* if you wish.

4 cloves garlic
1½ lb potatoes, chopped
4 cups water or Chicken
  *Stock**
1 bay leaf

½ teaspoon saffron
  strands
⅔ cup whipping cream
salt and pepper to taste

Serves 4
Preparation time:
20 minutes
Cooking time:
25–30 minutes
Freezing:
Not recommended

1. Place the garlic, potatoes, water, or stock, bay leaf and saffron in a large saucepan. Bring to the boil, then add salt and pepper. Cover and simmer for 25–30 minutes, until the potatoes are tender. Discard the bay leaf.
2. Puree in a blender or food processor, return to the pan and check the seasoning. Add the cream and reheat gently.

PEA AND HAM SOUP

1 ham bone, weighing about 1½ lb	*2 celery sticks, chopped*
½ lb yellow or green split peas, soaked overnight	*1 bouquet garni*
	6 cups water
	⅔ cup milk
1 large onion, chopped	*pepper to taste*

1. Place the ham bone, peas, onion, celery, bouquet garni and water in a large pan. Bring slowly to the boil, skim the surface, then cover and simmer for 2½ hours, until the peas are mushy and the ham is tender.

2. Discard the bouquet garni. Remove the ham bone from the pan, strip off all the meat and cut into small pieces.

3. Return the meat to the pan, add the milk and plenty of pepper and bring back to the boil. Serve piping hot.

Serves 4–6
Preparation time:
20 minutes, plus
soaking time
Cooking time:
2½ hours
Freezing:
Recommended

SPICED LENTIL SOUP

1 cup red lentils
3 celery sticks, chopped
2 carrots, chopped
5 cups Vegetable Stock*
⅓ cup bulgur wheat
2 tablespoons salad oil
1 onion, chopped
1 tablespoon chopped fresh
*   root ginger*

1 teaspoon cumin seeds
2 teaspoons ground
*   coriander*
½ teaspoon turmeric
1 tablespoon lemon juice
6 tablespoons Greek yogurt
salt and pepper to taste

Serves 6
Preparation time:
20 minutes
Cooking time:
35 minutes
Freezing:
Recommended

1. Place the lentils, celery, carrots and stock in a saucepan, bring to the boil, then cover and simmer for 15 minutes. Stir in the bulgur wheat, then simmer for 15 minutes.
2. Meanwhile, heat the oil in a small pan, add the onion and fry until lightly browned. Add the ginger and cumin seeds and fry for 5 minutes. Stir in the coriander and turmeric and cook for 1 minute.
3. Stir the spices into the soup. Check the seasoning. Simmer for 5 minutes then stir in the lemon juice. Serve hot, in bowls, with a spoonful of yogurt.

SALSIFY AND LEMON SOUP

Salsify is a long thin tapering root vegetable with a delicate flavor. Lemon not only helps it to keep its color but brings out its flavor too.

5 cups Chicken or
*   Vegetable Stock**
3 tablespoons lemon juice
1½ lb salsify
2 tablespoons chopped
*   celery leaves*

1 onion, chopped
1 teaspoon paprika
½ bunch watercress,
*   chopped finely*
⅔ cup whipping cream
salt and pepper to taste

Serves 4
Preparation time:
30 minutes
Cooking time:
45–55 minutes
Freezing:
Recommended

1. Place the stock and lemon juice in a large pan. Peel the salsify and cut into 3 inch lengths, adding to the pan as you work.
2. Add the celery leaves, onion, paprika, and salt and pepper. Bring to the boil, then cover and simmer for 40–50 minutes, until the salsify is tender.
3. Puree in a blender or food processor and return to the pan. Add the watercress and cream and simmer for 5 minutes. Check the seasoning. Serve hot.

LEEK AND OATMEAL SOUP

A little oatmeal added to this winter soup makes it even more substantial and gives it a sweet, slightly nutty taste.

2 tablespoons butter
1 onion, chopped
2 strips bacon, chopped
1 lb leeks, sliced
¼ cup fine oatmeal
4 cups Vegetable Stock*

1¼ cups milk
2 tablespoons chopped
  parsley
¾ cup grated Cheddar
  cheese
salt and pepper to taste

Serves 4
Preparation time:
20 minutes
Cooking time:
30 minutes
Freezing:
Not recommended

1. Melt the butter in a large saucepan, add the onion and bacon and fry for about 5 minutes. Stir in the leeks and cook for 2–3 minutes. Add the oatmeal and stir well.
2. Stir in the stock, bring to the boil, then cover and simmer for 20 minutes. Puree in a blender or food processor, return to the pan, add the milk, parsley, and salt and pepper and reheat thoroughly.
3. Just before serving, stir in the cheese. Remove from the heat and continue stirring until the cheese has melted. Serve with warm whole wheat rolls.

CARROT AND CELERIAC SOUP

1 tablespoon salad oil
1 tablespoon butter or
margarine
2 onions, grated
2¹/₂ cups grated carrot
2¹/₂ cups peeled and grated
celeriac
4 cups Chicken Stock*
1 teaspoon soy sauce

1 teaspoon grated orange
rind
2 tablespoons freshly
squeezed orange juice
²/₃ cup plain yogurt
2 teaspoons cornstarch
blended with 1
tablespoon water
chopped celery leaves to
garnish

1. Heat the oil and butter or margarine in a large sauce-pan, add the onions, carrot and celeriac and stir well. Lower the heat, cover the pan and allow the vegetables to sweat for 5 minutes.

2. Add the stock, bring to the boil, then cover and simmer for 20 minutes. Add the soy sauce, orange rind and juice and simmer for 10 minutes.

3. Mix the yogurt into the blended cornstarch. Stir into the soup and simmer for 5 minutes, stirring constantly.

4. Sprinkle with celery leaves and serve with Cheese Sticks* or fingers of toast.

Serves 4
Preparation time:
20 minutes
Cooking time:
40 minutes
Freezing:
Not recommended

VEGETABLE STOCK

This is a wonderful way of using up all those peelings you would normally throw away. The resulting stock is full of flavor and ideal for all vegetarian dishes, particularly risottos and main meal soups. Scrub the vegetables carefully before you peel them to remove any surface dirt.

*1/2–3/4 lb vegetable
    peelings, e.g. potato,
    carrot, turnip, rutabaga
few outer leaves from
    cabbage, lettuce, etc.
1 large onion, chopped*

*1 celery stick, chopped
1 bouquet garni
6 black peppercorns
2 bay leaves
7 1/2 cups cold water
salt and pepper to taste*

Makes about 6 cups
Preparation time:
10 minutes
Cooking time:
1–1 1/2 hours
Freezing:
Recommended

1. Place all the ingredients in a large saucepan and bring to the boil. Simmer, uncovered, for 1–1 1/2 hours, until the vegetables are very tender.
2. Strain into a large bowl and leave to cool. Use as required.

CHICKEN STOCK

*1 chicken carcass
7 1/2 cups cold water
1 onion, quartered
few celery leaves
strip lemon rind*

*1 carrot, chopped
2 cloves
1 bouquet garni
6 peppercorns
salt to taste*

Makes about 5 cups
Preparation time:
15 minutes
Cooking time:
2 hours
Freezing:
Recommended

1. Break up the chicken carcass and place in a large saucepan with the remaining ingredients. Bring to the boil, then cover and simmer for 2 hours.
2. Strain into a bowl and leave to cool. When cold remove any surface fat with paper towels. Use as required.

CROUTONS. Use white or whole wheat bread. Slice, then cut into 1/4–1/2 inch cubes or into small shapes using pastry cutters, e.g. hearts, stars. Fry in a little hot butter or oil for 4–5 minutes, until crisp and golden. Use to garnish soups.

COUNTRY RUSKS. Use whole wheat or white rolls. Pull the rolls apart and place broken side up on a baking sheet. Bake in a 400°F oven for 10–15 minutes, until crisp and browned. Serve warm with substantial soups or patés.

HOT CHEESE BREAD

1 small onion, grated	*1 cup finely grated Gruyère*
1 tablespoon chopped	*cheese*
parsley	*pepper to taste*
⅓ cup butter, softened	*1 long loaf of French bread*

1. Mix together the onion, parsley, butter, cheese and pepper until evenly blended.
2. Cut the loaf at 1 inch intervals almost to the base. Spread the cut sides with the cheese mixture. Wrap in foil.
3. Bake in a 400°F oven for 15 minutes, until the cheese has melted. Serve piping hot.

Serves 4–6
Preparation time:
15 minutes
Cooking time:
15 minutes
Freezing:
Recommended, at end of stage 2

CHEESE STICKS

½ lb ready-made puff	*½ cup grated Parmesan*
pastry	*cheese*
beaten egg for brushing	*salt, pepper and paprika to*
	taste

1. Roll out the pastry on a floured surface to 12 × 6 inches. Brush with egg and sprinkle with one-third of the cheese, and salt, pepper and paprika.
2. Fold the bottom third of the pastry up and the top third of the pastry down to cover it. Seal the edges.
3. Give the dough a quarter turn and roll out as before, sprinkling with half of the remaining cheese and the seasonings.
4. Roll out the dough to 12 × 8 inches. Brush with egg and sprinkle with the remaining cheese and seasonings.
5. Cut the dough into ½ inch wide strips from one short end. Twist the strips, place on dampened baking sheets and brush with egg.
6. Bake in a 425°F oven for 10–12 minutes, until risen and golden. Cool on a rack. Serve warm.

Makes 24
Preparation time:
20 minutes
Cooking time:
10–12 minutes
Freezing:
Recommended

INDEX

Almond and grape soup, chilled 18
Artichokes with mushrooms and Parma ham 26
Artichokes, marinated, with salami 26
Asparagus with cream and almonds 30
Asparagus and egg tarts 30
Avocado:
  Minted avocado dip 24
  Hot broiled avocado 52

Barbecued ribs 69
Broccoli soup with yogurt 20

Camembert puff pie with cranberry and port relish 70
Carrot and celeriac soup 77
Carrot and herb salad 10
Catalan soup, chilled 41
Celeriac:
  Carrot and celeriac soup 77
  Celeriac with egg and tarragon dressing 44
Cheese bread, hot 79
Cheese sticks 79
Chicken:
  Chicken liver and mushroom paté 68
  Chicken liver and sage crostini 50
  Chicken saté 16
  Chicken stock 78
  Indonesian chicken soup 58
  Warm chicken liver salad 68
  Watercress and chicken soup 22
Country garden tarts 64
Country rusks 79
Croutons 78
Crudités with mustard mayonnaise 28

Eggplant and tahini puree 44

Garlic-baked peppers with olives 42
Gingered shrimp 32
Gnocchi, green, with tomato sauce 48

Goats' cheese, baked, with salad 70
Greek cheese parcels, broiled 50
Green beans Provence-style 29

Ham:
  Potted ham with parsley 16
  Zucchini and ham stir-fry 8
Herb soup, Country 38
Herbed yogurt cheese 26

Late summer salad 24
Leek and oatmeal soup 76
Leek parcels, steamed 62
Lemon sole baked in a paper case 54
Lentil soup, spiced 74
Lentil-stuffed vine leaves 62
Lettuce and chervil soup 36

Minted avocado dip 24
Minted pea soup 22
Mushroom:
  Hot garlic mushrooms 46
  Stuffed mushrooms 60
Mussel:
  Baked mussels 66

Pakoras with mint chutney 46
Parsnip soup, spiced 72
Pea:
  Pea and ham soup 73
  Minted pea soup 22
Peppers, garlic-baked, with olives 42
Pork:
  Barbecued ribs 69
Potato and garlic soup 72
Potato skins, fried 60
Potted ham with parsley 16
Pumpkin soup 56

Red onion soup 58

Salsify and lemon soup 74
Sashimi 32
Scallops, skewered, with bacon 66
Seashells 52
Shortcrust pastry 64
Shrimp:
  Creamy shrimp pots 14

Gingered shrimp 32
Malaysian shrimp soup 20
Sorrel roulade with shrimp 12
Smoked haddock soup 54
Smoked mackerel and orange salad 10
Smoked salmon and asparagus terrine 12
Smoked salmon whirls 34
Smoked trout puree with fresh tomato sauce 34
Sole roll-ups with almond sauce 15
Sorrel roulade with shrimp 12
Spinach:
  Wilted spinach and egg salad 11
Stilton, celery and apple soup 56
Stock 78

Tagliatelle with pecan and parsley sauce 48
Tomato:
  Chilled tomato and basil soup 40
  Italian baked tomatoes 42

Vegetables. See also Artichokes etc.
  Spring vegetable soup with pesto 18
  Spring vegetables with warm mint dressing 6
  Vegetable stock 78
  Vegetables with green sauce 28
Vine leaves, lentil-stuffed 62

Watercress and chicken soup 22
Watercress and leek soup 38

Yogurt:
  Broccoli soup with yogurt 20
  Herbed yogurt cheese 36

Zucchini:
  Zucchini and ham stir-fry 8
  Zucchini soufflés 8

Photography by: Charlie Stebbings
Designed by: Sue Storey
Home economist: Mary Cadogan
Stylist: Penny Legg
Illustration by: Linda Smith
U.S. Consultant Editor: Carla Capalbo